Table of Contents

101

Getting Ready to Launch

1

You are about to embark on one of the defining journeys of your life – going to college, where you will discover, create, inspire, be inspired, and have a whole lot of fun. When you complete your degree – really it's not that far off – you may well be prepared to assist in the design of the first interplanetary spacecraft, write the next great American novel, or contribute to the health and well-being of people around the world. You will have gained confidence, developed self-reliance, built a circle of friends you'll cherish for years to come, created countless memories, and, if you're lucky, found the love of your life. You will have worked hard to succeed in college, and as you're about to learn, you'll have to work hard to get there.

Students, while your family should be involved in these processes, YOU should do the majority of the work.

Getting to college is a process that requires lots of learning, planning, and doing. *College Prep 101* is written to help with all these steps. After all, the more you know about the process, the easier it should be. *College Prep 101* covers most of the things you'll have to think about and the steps you'll have to take to get into college – investigating schools that interest you, choosing which ones to apply to, taking SATs and ACTs, applying for admission, and financing your higher education.

That's not the whole story, however. After you've decided which college you'll attend, you still need to know how to hit the ground running when you arrive on campus. *College Prep 101* also covers the transition to college – laying a foundation for college-level work with sound study skills and time management habits, and preparing for the personal choices every college student has to make.

As we set out, remember that the process of choosing and enrolling in a college should not be taken lightly. To make the smartest choices and the best transition to college, you'll need to devote time, attention, and energy. The next several years of your life, and the foundation of your professional life, depend on it.

Family Support

Also realize at the outset that you're not alone. Your family, particularly your parents or guardians, will be with you every step of the way. For this reason, *College Prep 101* is intended as a resource for parents too.

Parents, I encourage you read *College Prep 101* so you also know what to expect and can help your child prepare for what's around the corner. Your role ideally will be that of helper, guide, and sounding board. Your child can take a big step toward self-discipline and responsibility by taking the lead in the process. Encourage them to navigate the transition to college themselves, and you can move them further in that direction. Of course, your child will need to talk, so you should plan on doing a lot of listening. Ask lots of open-ended questions, and let them talk about what they want to talk about.

You can let them know about informational resources you find – and let them decide whether to use them. You can keep track of critical deadlines your child must meet and, instead of reminding them, discuss their progress toward meeting these deadlines. You can offer to share your thoughts about an admission or scholarship essay or suggest another reader rather than making your child hand it to you for editing.

In short, talk them through the things you used to do for them, give suggestions where you used to help, and leave them on their own where you used to make suggestions.

Obviously, you'll need to have a conversation with your child to prepare them for your new approach, but if you explain that it's just a way to ease them into the major changes they'll encounter when they get to college, and that you'll still be there if they need your help, it should be okay.

Students, Take the Lead

Students, while your family should be involved in these processes, YOU should do the majority of the work. Let them help you remember deadlines, prepare for tests,

type applications, practice admission interview questions, etc. You should also take them with you on some of your campus visits – they need to feel comfortable with the school you choose too!

Enough said by way of introduction. On to the important stuff!

Planning for College

CHECKLISTS & CALENDARS

2

As a high school student, you'll have lots of steps to take on the way to college. This chapter includes a number of checklists you can use to make sure you take the right steps. Plus we'll discuss the all-important calendar for your busy final year in high school.

First though, let's get real. Not everyone starts thinking about college as a 14-year-old freshman, even though it's a good idea. If that's you, or you get this book later in your high school career, do your best to complete each step anyway. After all, the final goal is the same.

All Four Years

- ☐ Enroll in a college preparatory curriculum.
- ☐ Get involved in extracurricular activities.
- ☐ Volunteer in your community.
- ☐ Explore careers that interest you and job opportunities in those careers.
- ☐ Study hard and do well in school.
- ☐ Attend events on college campuses – plays, concerts, sporting events, activities related to your possible major, and more.
- ☐ Get to know your high school counselor – your college or senior counselor, that is; let them get to know you and your goals, career aspirations, schools you're considering, etc. Your parents may want to go along too.
- ☐ Talk to friends about their plans for college and careers; talk to your parents and your friends' parents about THE REAL WORLD.
- ☐ Start a college savings account, make regular deposits, and resist withdrawals.

It's never too early to start preparing for college.
Your freshman year is when your grades become part of a permanent academic record that colleges look at when considering you for admission.

FRESHMAN

Small List

- [ ] It's never too early to start preparing for college. Your freshman year is when your grades become part of a permanent academic record that colleges look at when considering you for admission.
- [ ] Write papers and do projects about college whenever possible.
- [ ] Enter essay contests, speech competitions, science fairs, and the like for scholarships and awards.
- [ ] Talk with your counselor about the PLAN and PSAT tests and when to take them

SOPHOMORE

Big List

- [ ] Read the "College Entrance Exams" chapter in this book.
- [ ] Take the PLAN Test.
- [ ] Take the PSAT Test in October to practice for next year's PSAT, which will count toward scholarships.
- [ ] Go online and start looking at college web sites, sign up for podcasts, etc.
- [ ] Attend college fairs that come to your area; get all the free information you can.
- [ ] Get a job, even if your last name is Gates or Trump and you don't have to – it'll show you're hard-working and responsible.
- [ ] "Job shadow" someone with a job you'd like to do (that means you follow them around for a day).

JUNIOR

Bigger List

- [ ] Keep working hard. This year's academic record will go a long way toward helping or hurting your chances of getting into your schools of choice; if you've been slacking, you can make up a lot of ground this year.

- [ ] Read and digest the "Choosing a College" chapter in this book!

- [ ] Volunteer to help a senior dig up scholarship information – and make a deal that you get to keep the information when they're done.

- [ ] Reread the "College Entrance Exams" chapter in this book – before you take your tests!

- [ ] Take the PSAT in October; this one is to qualify for National Merit Scholarship Competition, and it can be very important.

- [ ] Attend an ACT/SAT preparation workshop, or if you can't, purchase practice books, software, etc. to help you prepare.

- [ ] Take the ACT and/or SAT in the spring; this way you'll have at least one score going into your senior year; it also puts you on schools' mailing lists and provides schools you are considering with significant information about you.

- [ ] Investigate colleges, request information, download whatever you can.

- [ ] Visit college campuses and take tours, visit with advisors and faculty, pick up admission packets, and get a feel for college life.

- [ ] Take solid elective courses, especially in fields related to your possible major – e.g., extra math, science, foreign language, social science, computer courses, etc.

- [ ] Talk with friends and family to gather ideas about colleges.

- [ ] Run for leadership positions in the organizations you're involved in.
- [ ] Ask your high school counselor for suggestions about colleges you should consider but might not have thought of.
- [ ] Find out the admission criteria for your top schools, know where you stand in relation to those requirements, and work toward improving if necessary.

The All-Important Calendar

After your junior year, you should purchase a large wall calendar that displays an entire year at a time, preferably the academic year, and post it in a place where you and your parents can see it. Using a different color pen for each of your potential schools, mark admission, scholarship, financial aid, and other deadlines on the appropriate dates. Mark dates for ACT and SAT tests, as well as other important dates. By doing this and posting it where the family can see it, you'll be involving them in the process.

Of course, living in the digital age, you might be able to sync your calendar with your parents' on your computers, BlackBerrys, and iPhones. If this works for you, do it, so long as everyone can view and share what you're doing. If you're not sure of the technology, opt for the good old wall model.

SENIOR

Extreme List

> **During your senior year, work even harder and challenge yourself; you don't want a blow-off schedule.**

- [ ] Work even harder, continuing to challenge yourself and take solid elective courses; trust me, you don't want to take a blow-off schedule. If you fall out of your good study habits, your first year of college will probably be more difficult.
- [ ] Read the "Choosing a College" chapter again.
- [ ] Attend college fairs in your area.
- [ ] Visit college campuses – visit many, and visit often; attend events at the colleges you're interested in.
- [ ] Visit friends at college, and find out what they like and dislike.
- [ ] Talk with people whose opinions you respect about the schools you're considering.

EARLY FALL

- [ ] Gather applications to the schools you are considering, and use your calendar to note deadlines for applications, scholarships, housing, etc.
- [ ] Sit down with everyone who has a stake in your college decision and listen to their input.
- [ ] Ask people to write letters of recommendation for you; choose people who actually know you, not just those with cool titles, and give them plenty of time.
- [ ] Borrow scholarship information – contacts, addresses, applications, etc. – from someone a year ahead of you who received several scholarships and/or had the same major.
- [ ] Understand the admission criteria for your top schools, know where you stand, and improve what you can if necessary.
- [ ] Re-read the "College Entrance Exams" chapter – before you take the tests!

- [ ] Take the ACT/SAT in September/October, and repeat as necessary or desired.
- [ ] Read "The Application Process" chapter in this book.
- [ ] Apply for early admission if appropriate.

MID-FALL

- [ ] Talk to your high school counselor about scholarships awarded by local organizations, get the applications, and keep checking back for the latest information (without driving your counselor nuts).
- [ ] Apply for admission to the colleges of your choice.
- [ ] Read the "College and Money" chapter in this book.
- [ ] Apply for scholarships before Christmas break if the application deadline isn't earlier.
- [ ] Verify the arrival of your applications, transcripts, etc.; some schools have an online system that provides these updates, or you can call the admissions office and ask.

WINTER/SPRING

- [ ] Attend a financial aid workshop with your parents.
- [ ] Apply for financial aid as soon after January 1 as possible, and be sure to remind your parents to complete the FAFSA as soon as possible.
- [ ] Take CLEP/AP Tests, if applicable.
- [ ] Go back for a second or third visit to campuses you're considering.
- [ ] It's time to make a decision!

TIP

If you think you fall a bit short of academic requirements, apply early — a provisional admission program could be your ticket in.

As Soon As You Choose A

SCHOOL

- ☐ Apply for housing. If you're still trying to decide between a couple of schools, you may need to apply for housing at both – this will be expensive though.
- ☐ Get familiar with your college and what you'll need when you get there, including:
  - ▶▶ Housing options – on-campus, off-campus, Greek, etc.
  - ▶▶ Course selection and scheduling.
  - ▶▶ Faculty and programs in your major.
  - ▶▶ Do you need a car? If so, where will you park?
  - ▶▶ Do you need a bike?
  - ▶▶ Should you have your own computer? Desktop or laptop?

PARENTS

Checklist

- ☐ Read the "College and Money" chapter in this book, and do your best to plan ahead for college finances.
- ☐ Discuss the college process with your child regularly, and let him or her make most of the decisions.
- ☐ Visit schools with your child; let them take the lead and visit again – without you.
- ☐ Organize a group of parents to meet and talk about your children going to college; you're likely to appreciate the support.
- ☐ Make your child do the work of searching for schools, applying, etc.; help them but don't do it for them. They'll be more invested in the process and its results.
- ☐ In your child's senior year, do your taxes ASAP after January 1 so you can submit financial aid applications early (they use some of the same information).
- ☐ Visit **http://fafsa.ed.gov** to learn more.

Choosing a College

Choosing a college is one of the first truly major decisions you will make in your life. Your choice will have far-reaching effects on virtually every aspect of your life. Going to the wrong school won't put you in the poor house for the rest of your life, but at different schools you'll meet different people, be involved in different activities, develop different areas of your self, interview with different companies, etc. All of these variables, and many others, help determine the direction you will take after college.

While it's unlikely that the school you choose will drastically affect the success you achieve, your life will clearly be different based on where you attend college. Consider two scenarios:

Five years after receiving your engineering degree from College A, you might be a production engineer for General Motors making $80,000 per year, live in Detroit with your spouse – the love of your life whom you met in college – and two children, and donate money annually to the fraternity or sorority you were a member of.

Five years after completing your engineering degree at College B, you might be single, a process engineer for ConocoPhillips making $80,000 per year, living in Houston, dating and actively searching for the love of your life, and volunteering a good deal of your time in your community.

As you can see, in both situations, you have a good life, but the point is that the two lives are very different. In order to make the best possible decision as to which college to attend, it is important to have a plan.

My years as a college recruiter gave me a lot of insight into the school search process, and the following suggestions may serve you well in your personal hunt. And remember that choosing colleges to apply to is a process, not a checklist, so flexibility is key. Ideally, you'll work through this process during the junior year of high school.

Gather Info

Read through the mail/e-mail you receive from colleges, and request more information from those you're interested in. Keep an open mind about all the schools you investigate. Talk about college with parents, friends, and other family members – about specific schools and about personal experiences with college.

Start writing down what you are looking for in a college, and don't worry if you're unsure. In my experience asking hundreds of students what they were looking for in a college, most didn't know. Beyond big or small, and close to home or far away, your thoughts may be difficult to put into words. But keep at it. It's a thinking process, and you have a lot of thinking and learning to do before you make a decision.

Make a Wish List

Make a wish list of colleges. Think on both a grand scale and on the most basic level. List all the schools you think you might like to attend, from the school on the beach or in the mountains to the one with the best academic reputation in your projected major. And don't forget the school down the street, possibly a junior or community college. After all, it would be significantly less expensive and closer to home. Remember this is a wish list, so include any school. Cost should not be a limitation at this point.

It's wise to include a range of schools in your list. Life isn't entirely predictable, and those with a backup plan are usually much better off than those without. You might plan to go away to college or to a fairly expensive school, but then you might change your mind at the last minute – or be forced to. Too many times I've seen students scrambling to change their college choice because they realize what it will be like coming home only at Christmas or figure out how long it will take to pay off $30,000 a year in college loans, not to mention the possibility of parental job loss or other financial problems, significant health problems suffered by close family members, unexpected illness or injury suffered by yourself, or even a family move. Some students will even change their college choice to stay close to a boyfriend/girlfriend. Long story short, have a backup plan!

Life isn't entirely predictable, and those with a backup plan are usually much better off than those without.

Expect your parents to have at least a mental wish list for you. They'll probably include some or all of the following – the school down the street, their alma mater, and Harvard, Yale, or Stanford. Consider adding their schools to your list.

After you've spoken with a number of people about colleges and made up your wish list, sit down with everyone who has a stake in your college decision. Usually, this will just be your immediate family, including siblings, even the little ones, relatives or others who might be helping you pay for college, as well as a spouse or fiancé. Talk realistically about the schools on your list. Consider academic reputation, quality of their program in your anticipated major, cost, distance from home, student life, safety, support system, etc. Let everyone offer their opinions, and be open to both pros and cons of all the schools, even those that are on your list only to please others. Be sure to take notes so you'll remember what was said.

Narrow Your List

After hearing what everyone else thinks, wait a few days, then narrow down your list. Eliminate schools that aren't realistic based on your grades and standardized test scores, affordability (although you should remember that if you really want to go to school somewhere but it seems financially out of reach, there is money available through financial aid programs), or whatever variables are applicable to you. It is important to note that starting at one institution and later transferring to another happens often.

You should be able to narrow your choices down to between three and six colleges. Some of you may not even have started with six; others will have difficulty narrowing down to ten. That's fine. Your final decision won't come till much later, after you've visited the schools, applied to them, received scholarship or financial aid awards, etc.

As you narrow your list, you'll need to consider all the pros and cons for each school, even the intangible feeling you get when you visit. Don't forget that the way you are treated during the application process, good or bad, is probably the way you will be treated once you go to school there.

After you narrow your choices, apply to the schools, and visit, you should have a pretty good idea where you fit best. Hopefully you will not have to make your decision based entirely on finances, but if you have two or three equal favorites, you may have to.

School Reputations

An important issue to note is the belief that the name of the school you attend somehow makes you more or less attractive to employers. Don't spend too much time being concerned with which school has the biggest name (this is particularly true if you intend to go to graduate school). Employers are likely more interested in exactly what you can do for their bottom line than what school you attended. Can you make them money? Can you design or sell their products? Can you do it better than other people they've interviewed?

Know Yourself

During the process of selecting a college to attend, you are also doing a great deal of self-analysis. Who you are should be one of the most important factors in selecting the right school. The degree to which you are able to figure out what you like and don't like, the kind of setting you are most comfortable in, the kinds of people you want to go to school with, among other things, will have a direct impact on your happiness and success in college.

You are not only trying to figure out what you like and what situation will best allow you to succeed, you are also trying to figure out why.

In getting to know yourself, you are not only trying to figure out what you like and what situation will best allow you to succeed, you are also trying to figure out why. Let's say you want to go to college in Florida. You need to understand why that's your desire. If it's because you live in Florida, or have confidence in the Florida higher education system, or want to major in marine biology, you probably have a good reason. If it's because you like lots of sunshine and time at the beach, or you live in Washington State and Florida is as far as you can get from your ex, you probably aren't considering the best reasons. So as you start to determine what your preferences are, be sure to ask yourself why they are your preferences.

To get a start at knowing yourself, ask these questions:

▶ What type of location am I looking for in a school? Small town or big city? Close to home or far away? Mountains? Sunshine? Proximity to outdoor recreation?

▶ What type of school am I looking for? Large or small? Public or private? Junior college of four-year school? Liberal arts, technical, or comprehensive?

▶ What type of philosophical base does the college and its student body have? Progressive? Politically active? Religious? Conservative? Liberal? Diverse?

▶ Does it matter what type of extracurricular activities are available at a school? Leadership opportunities? Intramural sports? Music, theater, and arts? Fraternities and sororities? Athletic programs?

▶ Am I willing to take on financial debt to attend one school over another, less expensive one? Loans? Part-time employment?

▶ Does it matter if I know anyone, or if any of my friends attend the college I choose?

||| College Entrance Exams

4

The most stress-inducing part of the college preparation process is standardized testing. Unfortunately for some, this stress actually affects their ability to do well on the tests, thus impacting admission and/or scholarship decisions at some schools. The information presented here is intended to familiarize you with the two most common college admission tests – SAT and ACT – and provide helpful hints to ensure that your score accurately reflects your knowledge and abilities. It is intended only as a supplement to other test preparation materials and programs, but I do think if you read this information and follow the suggestions, you'll eliminate many of the pitfalls that negatively affect students' scores.

Standardized tests are designed to measure knowledge in areas predetermined to predict academic success in college, not how smart a student is.

The two most common college admission tests are the SAT, produced by the College Board, and the ACT, produced by the ACT Corporation. Neither is an intelligence or IQ test, and their scores do not indicate how smart a student is. The tests are designed to measure knowledge in areas predetermined to predict academic success in college. Colleges use test scores alongside high school grades and a variety of other factors to try to identify students with the highest potential or probability for success.

Students should realize the importance of the tests, but not place undue burdens on themselves to achieve because of them. Every year, students are admitted to schools in spite of lower scores than they would have liked. These students usually did very well in high school, wrote excellent application essays, were leaders among their peers, or had exceptional talents in other areas. Conversely, students whose applications may be lacking in other areas but have exceptional test scores are also admitted regularly. Students who fare the best around college admission time and have the most options are those who work hard, take a solid college preparatory curriculum and perform well, become active in their school and community, prepare for and do well on college admission tests, and pursue outside interests.

Below you'll find general test preparation information common to both tests and answers to frequently asked questions. Information specific to each test is best left to the experts and the people who put the tests together in the first place.

Getting Started

There are two places to learn about and sign up for standardized tests:

▶ Your high school counselor will have test registration booklets for both tests that include example test questions you should review. Your counselor may also have review books, videos, computer programs, or other resources for your use.

▶ The Internet is home to tons of useful resources. The first web sites to visit are the homes of the SAT – **www.collegeboard.org** – and ACT – **www.act. org**. Both provide a great deal of information, offer their own preparation products, and recommend additional resources. You can also sign up for each test on that company's web site.

WHEN ARE THE TESTS OFFERED?

During the academic year, the SAT is offered seven times, beginning in October, while the ACT is offered six times, beginning in September. Specific dates, as well as any date changes, are available on the SAT and ACT web sites.

TIP

Don't attach more significance to your score than is necessary – and don't do it to others' scores either.

HOW MUCH DO THE TESTS COST?

As of March 2007, the cost for taking the basic SAT is $43 and the ACT is $30. You may also want to invest in test preparation or similar services, and you may want to sign up for additional tests.

HOW LONG DO THE TESTS TAKE?

Both the ACT and SAT take about four hours, including a number of breaks between sections of the test.

Scoring High

Many of you will be wondering what a good score is. There is no definitive answer to this one, since the definition of a "good" score will vary from person to person. Still, it's a very good idea to work toward the best possible scores you can achieve.

Perfect scores – 36 on the ACT, 1600 on the SAT – are rarely achieved, and are the result of extremely good preparation over an entire school career. Depending on your age, year in school, the high school you attend, how many times you take the test, and many other factors, what you consider only an okay score might be a very good score in someone else's eyes. Try to avoid comparing yourself to others based on these test scores. Don't attach more significance to your score than is necessary – and don't do it to others' scores either.

HOW CAN I MAKE SURE I DO MY BEST?

PREPARE

▶ Take practice tests and read the information available on the ACT and SAT web sites.

TAKE

▶ A watch, digital if possible. At the start of each test section, set it to 12:00, or 00:00, to keep track of time remaining. Set any alarms to silent.

▶ A calculator, but only one you're familiar with. You don't want to waste any time figuring out how to use the thing. Calculators are permitted, but it's still a good idea to check the ACT or SAT web site for any restrictions.

▶ Take an official photo ID and your test admission information/slip.

▶ Take several sharpened #2 lead pencils, not mechanical pencils.

▶ Take plenty of Kleenex if you have a cough or runny nose.

▶ Take snacks for breaks between test sections. SAT encourages you to do so. But ACT doesn't mention snacking that I know of, so when you arrive ask if snacking is okay; if not, then don't.

GET SET

▶ Relax.

▶ Get plenty of rest the night before the test.

▶ Eat a good breakfast.

- ▶ Dress comfortably and in layers in case the room is hot or cold.
- ▶ Arrive 15 minutes early but not more than that – testing centers rarely open earlier.

GO

- ▶ Pace yourself, and don't spend too much time on any one question.
- ▶ Know the instructions and format for each section.
- ▶ Answer the questions you know first.
- ▶ Check your work if time allows.
- ▶ Be careful on the answer sheet. Mark answer ovals completely, and erase changes completely.
- ▶ Guess when appropriate: ACT recommends you answer every question because there is no penalty for incorrect answers: **www.actstudent.org/testprep/tips/index.html**. SAT recommends making educated guesses when you can eliminate one or more of the available choices and skipping questions you can't answer: **www.collegeboard.com/student/ testing/sat/prep_one/test_tips.html**.
- ▶ On reading sections of tests, read the questions before reading the passage. You'll then know what to look for in the passage.
- ▶ Be cautious of questions or possible answers that contain superlatives or extreme answers, e.g., *always, never, all, only*; absolute qualifiers demand absolute answers.

Your Score

You'll receive a score report from SAT or ACT about a month after your test. Or go online to view your scores. Both the College Board and ACT post most scores online about two-and-a-half weeks after the test. You might also be able to receive your score more quickly for an extra fee; check the SAT or ACT web site for availability and details.

Test Again

Take and retake the tests. Most schools will accept your highest score, and most if not all will accept either test, regardless of how many times you take it.

Also take the PSAT/NMSQT or PLAN tests in tenth and/ or eleventh grade to prepare for the SAT or ACT, identify your potential weaknesses, and inform schools that you are interested in them.

> Take and retake the tests. Most schools will accept your highest score... regardless of how many times you take it.

The Application Process

5

The application process is one of the crucial steps in selecting a college. While filling out and submitting applications to your chosen schools may seem like a one-time activity, it is actually a very fluid process with multiple steps spread out over time. There is some overlap between this chapter and the "Choosing a College" and "College and Money" chapters, although this chapter expands on common topics and presents a more complete view of the process plus helpful hints to make it easier.

Early in the fall of your senior year, you should start the process of applying to college. The process can be tedious and repetitive and can get overwhelming; you should not plan on doing it alone. Enlist the help of your high school counselor and your family. They should NOT do everything for you, but they will be able to make your job go much more smoothly. Your counselor and your family can help you remember deadlines, clarify how to answer certain questions, make copies, get transcripts, possibly assist with typing or entering text into online applications (don't ask your counselor for help with this one), and other tasks. Make sure to check with your counselor about any specific procedures or deadlines they may require. This way you can build their requirements into your application process. The steps outlined in this chapter should guide you through the process with a minimum of problems and headaches.

Don't try to decide where you'll go to school before you apply for admission.

Whatever you do, don't try to decide where you'll go to school before applying for admission. Apply to all the schools on your list. Your admissions application will act as a trigger for all the rest of the applications – financial aid, scholarships, housing, etc. – that you will submit. If you wait to apply for admission, you might miss out on certain scholarships and financial aid.

Step 1: Gather Applications

As your senior year begins, you should be gathering applications from the schools you are considering. Some may have already been sent to you, and many can be picked up in your counselor's office or at college fairs; you may have to request others directly from the school. Also, most colleges have applications that you download from their web sites or simply fill out and submit online. Since you are likely to receive unsolicited information from a number of colleges, make sure to keep the applications from the schools you are interested in separate from the rest. This will make them much easier to find when it comes time to fill them out.

Step 2: Know the Deadlines

Since you're probably considering several schools, knowing the deadlines is not as easy as it may sound. Each school has its own set of deadlines, as well as priority dates or other dates to remember. Applications received on or before the priority date get special consideration; those received after the date get no special handling.

This is a good opportunity to use the big wall calendar I recommended in the "Planning for College" chapter. Now is the time to keep track of all your dates and deadlines. Being organized will go a long way to help with the application process.

> **Keep track of all your dates and deadlines. Being organized will go a long way to help with the application process.**

Step 3: Apply for Admission

Although applying to schools can be an expensive proposition, depending on how many and which schools you are considering, it is important to apply early – during the fall of your senior year, preferably early fall. Some schools, particularly private schools and those with early admission policies, may in fact have early autumn deadlines, so be aware.

Be careful and be thorough filling out applications, whether on paper or online. Mistakes can cause you major headaches later on. The following suggestions should help you avoid many of those mistakes.

- Make a photocopy of each application, hand write your responses on the copy, and then type your responses on the real application.
- Make sure to fill out the entire application.
- Include official transcripts, along with anything else required, with each application. Official transcripts normally include all course work completed, standardized test scores, cumulative GPA, rank in class, and an official stamp or seal from your school, and usually have to be requested ahead of time.
- Always proofread applications before mailing. You'd be surprised how many people mistakenly indicate they have been convicted of a felony or give the wrong social security number.

Double-check the address on each envelope to make sure you don't put the application for one school in another school's envelope (yes, this has actually happened!). This can be a potential problem if you are applying to several schools and all at the same time.

Step 4: Apply for Financial Aid

Depending on several factors, including the scholarship deadlines of the schools you are considering and when

your parents' tax information is available to them, steps 4 and 5 can be switched. But do both as soon as possible. You can find more specific financial aid information in the chapter on "College and Money."

The most important thing to remember is that applying for financial aid is a separate process from applying for admission. There is a universal application, called the Free Application for Federal Student Aid (FAFSA), which everyone fills out and submits to a central processor. On the FAFSA, you can list up to six colleges that will receive your financial aid information. You do NOT have to decide which college you want to attend before applying for financial aid, and if you wait to apply for scholarships or aid, you might miss out.

The universal application for financial aid is available from every high school counselor and every college or university (check with the schools you are considering to see if they require any additional forms), as well as online at **www.fafsa.ed.gov**. The forms cannot be filled out before January 1, but should be filled out and submitted as soon as possible after that date. Check with your high school counselor or any college financial aid office for answers to specific questions.

Step 5: Apply for Scholarships

During the time you are applying for scholarships, you may also be applying for special programs such as an honors program and/or enrichment opportunities at your chosen schools. Usually, applications for these programs are similar to those for scholarships, and the same advice applies:

▶ Carefully, neatly, and accurately complete all portions of each application.
▶ Double and triple check your spelling. If possible, have someone else also check your spelling.

Always proofread applications before mailing. You might be surprised how many people mistakenly indicate they have been convicted of a felony or give the wrong social security number.

▶ Make copies before sending any applications in the mail or submitting them online.

Letters of recommendation are reviewed in a variety of ways by colleges. Some see them as a very valuable tool for use in evaluating applicants. Some take them with a grain of salt because they never say anything bad – you're obviously going to get letters from people who think highly of you. Either way, colleges want them, so you have to get them.

Apply early. Applying at the deadline leaves no margin for error.

▶ In choosing whom to ask for these letters, you should remember a few things. The recommender should be someone who knows you very well – if they have a neat title or are somehow important or influential, that's just icing on the cake. Vague recommendations from big name people rarely impress colleges. Rremember, they see thousands each year.

▶ Ask if they would be willing and have time to write a letter for you. Don't assume that they are just sitting around hoping you'll ask.

▶ Give the people writing your recommendations plenty of time to think about and write the letters. As you start gathering applications, you should be contacting the people you would like to write your letters. Tell them you're planning ahead and know you'll need letters later on, and ask if they'd be willing to write one at a later date. That way they have plenty of time to think about it, and you get to them before others do.

▶ Plan to give each person writing a recommendation a copy of your resume. No matter how well they know you they couldn't possibly know everything you've done.

After completing the steps listed above, it's time to start making some decisions. Before you move on to the next step in the process, you'll either need to be narrowing down your choices or making the financial commitment to pursue housing at a number of schools.

Step 6: Secure Housing

Securing a place to live – usually, campus housing for incoming freshmen – is the part of the application process that usually requires a significant outlay of cash, but because rooms are almost always assigned on a first come, first served basis, you can't afford to wait until you make your final decision. There is usually a fee to apply for campus housing, and there is almost always a fee to reserve a room. If you can afford to apply and reserve rooms at all of the schools you've been accepted to, go ahead. Usually, a portion of this money is refundable if you choose not to attend and notify them before a deadline. Otherwise reserve a room at your top choices. There is a bit of a gamble involved in this step – is it worth possibly losing your housing application fee if you don't go to school there? Just make sure you get a room.

Speed is usually the key. Campus housing fill up fast at many schools, so find out what it is like at the schools you're considering.

Step 7: Enroll and Attend Orientation

Soon after securing a room, if not before, you'll likely be entering the final decision phase. At this time, the only major activities remaining are enrolling and attending orientation. The way schools enroll their new students and provide orientations are so varied that there is very little universal information I can provide. Schools will communicate to you exactly when and where you need to be, but if you plan on two or three days during the summer for enrollment and three or four days just prior to the start of school for orientation, you'll be on the safe side. Do not underestimate the importance of orientation. There wouldn't be an orientation if you didn't need it!

Helpful Application Hints

▶ Make copies of everything before you send it or submit it online.

▶ Apply early. Applying before a deadline can help if you leave a question blank or forget to send a transcript or have another oversight – the school might have time to contact you to fix the problem before the deadline hits. Applying at the deadline leaves no margin for error.

▶ If you want to apply for admission to a school, but can't afford the application fee, check with your high school counselor or the admissions office at the college. Application fees can be waived in certain situations if there is financial need.

▶ Keep extra transcripts on hand, and plan to send one with all applications except those for campus housing.

▶ Work closely with your counselor. Make sure to keep in mind their busy schedule as well as any procedures they may require – remember you are only one of many students they work with.

▶ If possible, enroll on the first possible date. College basically runs on a first come, first served basis. This is particularly true with class times. You'll usually be able to take the same or similar classes if you enroll at a later date, but you might be going to those classes at 7:30 a.m. or at 3:30 p.m. on Friday.

▶ Some schools have an early decision or early admission window. These schools may have special requirements that I have not listed, or a special application process differing from what I have outlined. Some may have a special type of early admission policy that is binding, and may actually prevent you from applying to other schools. If this is the case, you need to know exactly what is required of you, and what special dates are applicable. You should contact each school you are considering to find out any requirements specific to that school.

Visiting College Campuses

You should plan to visit each of the schools you applied to beginning in the summer after your junior year in high school. And don't try to cram the process into too short a time span. Note also that visiting colleges can be a major commitment for the entire family – often expensive and time-consuming. But it is very important.

When you start planning your visits, make sure to go with friends or family members you can have fun with. I'm not encouraging you to leave your parents at home, but before you arrive you may want to discuss with them who will do the talking, what you'd like to do, etc. College visits are occasionally stressful, and students sometimes get hacked off or embarrassed by their parents. Do what you can to eliminate the possibility. It will make the visit much more pleasant, and if you don't have fun on your visit, you are much less likely to have a favorable impression of the school overall. Also, only as a last resort should you visit two colleges on the same day, as neither will get a fair shake. It will take at least half a day to see the campus and visit with all of the people you need to visit.

> **When you start planning your campus visits, make sure to go with friends or family members you can have fun with.**

Campus visits should be set up by the college's recruitment office – whether that's the admissions office, high school relations office, or prospective student services office – or by the representative who visited your school. They should be able to schedule you for a tour and arrange appointments with the appropriate people. In some situations, you may have to call a couple of different offices before you reach someone accustomed to setting up a number of appointments for a visitor.

You can do a number of things during a visit, and you should try to do as many of the following as is practical and you want to do:

▶ Take the organized campus tour, even if you've visited the campus before. Most tours include a look at a residence hall room, a look at the library, and at least a walk through an academic building– all are a must.

▶ Speak with representatives about the application process, financial aid, scholarships, etc., to see if you've done everything you need to. You may have to speak with different people about each subject. Speak with the representative who visited your school and others who have contacted you, even if its just to say hello. This will show your interest, maturity, and initiative.

- Sit in on a class. Watch how the professor teaches, how the students react, and how they interact with one another.

- Speak with an advisor, professor, or department head from your major (it's okay to visit more than one department if you're undecided about a major). These are the people you'll work with directly if you attend the school. They can tell you about the specific classes you will take, their facilities, potential careers, internships, etc.

- Spend the night on campus if possible. Things are sometimes different at night – the campus may be very busy or deserted. Some schools make rooms in campus housing available to visitors at a very affordable rate.

Spend the night on campus if possible. Things are sometimes different at night – the campus may be very busy or deserted.

- Attend a campus event. Most evenings on a college campus there are a number of things going on – a sporting event, variety show, play, concert, or other student activity.

- Plan some free time. Walking around a college campus by yourself is very fun, and usually will give you a good idea what you will feel like if you attend school there. In addition, you'll see a great deal more than what you see on a tour.

- People-watch. If you choose that school, you will be one of those people.

- Take notes on what people tell you, but don't write down everything. You'll be given far too much information to remember it all.

Additional Suggestions

- If you can, you should take copies of your transcript, application, letters of recommendation, and test scores. You probably won't need them, so it's all right to leave them in your car, but having them handy could really pay off if they've lost your original or need an additional copy.

- Don't monopolize people's time. They should be willing to speak with you if they are able, but be brief. They'll let you know if they can spare more than a few minutes.

▶ When you leave, make sure there is someone – an advisor, professor, recruiter, department head, etc. – who you know and who knows who you are. You've heard the phrase "It's who you know"; well sometimes, it's who knows you!

▶ When you return home, maintain contact with the people you've met. Call or write once a semester just to check in, and make sure you have completed everything you're supposed to. Make sure to re-introduce yourself and remind them where you're from.

▶ Even if you've been around a school quite a bit – attended athletic events, visited friends, etc. – resist the temptation to think you know everything you need to know. Rarely will you just pick up the important information, and sometimes you may pick up the wrong information unintentionally. Even friends who attend that school may give wrong information, not knowing that policies have changed.

▶ College recruitment weekends are a very valuable way to find out about a school, and may be able to take the place of an individual visit. Usually, the recruitment events are planned to be very fun, and give you a brief look at several aspects of their school, rather than an in-depth look at anything. Depending on the size of the group, you may or may not be able to get all of your questions answered. If not, and another visit is impractical, you may be able to get your questions answered via telephone, e-mail, or letter.

When you leave campus, make sure there is someone – an advisor, professor, recruiter, department head – who you know and who knows who you are.

College and Money

For most of you, and your families, money will be a pivotal factor in determining which colleges you apply to and which one you choose to attend. Tuition, fees, and living expenses at a top private school might add up to $35,000 per year, or $140,000 for a four-year school career. At many state universities, costs can exceed $15,000 per year, or $60,000 for a four-year program.

Money isn't the only factor of course, and you definitely shouldn't write off a school because you think you might not be able to afford it. There are many ways to get help paying for college. This chapter will try to touch the most important money bases – from college savings plans for students and parents to merit-based aid, need-based aid, and spending habits once you're away at school (money concerns don't magically end when you arrive at school and unpack you bags – far from it).

Students and parents should work together to plan and budget for college.

Before going any further, I believe it is important for students and parents to work together to plan and budget for college. An honest, open discussion about college costs and available resources can pave the way for fewer mistakes and misunderstandings later. You'd do well to talk about all the topics covered in this chapter, from college savings to emergencies at school. Students should know their responsibilities, how to fulfill them, and what to do if a mistake is made. Even if you parents have plenty of money to pay for college, your child might benefit from being responsible for some portion of their college expenses, whether books and supplies, fraternity dues, food above and beyond their food service contract, or cell phone bills.

This chapter is a little different from the rest in that it's addressed to both students and parents because paying for college and managing money once you're there usually depends on the whole family and impacts everyone as well. And a word of advice – I am not a financial expert, just someone who has seen every side of the college process. I strongly encourage you to consult a financial planner, particularly one who knows the ins and outs of the college money game.

Saving for College

When planning for college, whether as a student or parent, the most important first step is to SAVE MONEY. The earlier you start saving, the better – though it's never too late to start. Parents, your college savings account is, in and of itself, an important message to your child. If you don't plan ahead, how can you expect them to? No matter how big or small it might be, start an account and contribute regularly. Automatic fund transfers from your bank account to the college account are an excellent way to make contributions on a regular schedule. Also, 529 tax-sheltered college savings plans offer significant tax benefits. I suggest you consult an expert about this type of account.

Students, you should start saving for college as well – the sooner, the better. I always advise parents to make their children contribute to their college education by paying for some significant part of the overall expense – e.g., books and supplies, entertainment, food over and above any meal plan. You can sock away more money than you think by depositing a portion of any money you receive as birthday or other gifts, or getting a part-time job and committing yourself to putting half your pay – or more – into the bank. The goal is to make regular deposits and to resist the temptation to withdraw your money (you don't really need that iPhone, do you?) until you're away at school.

Financial Aid

Even if you've planned well ahead, your college savings accounts probably won't cover the total cost of four years or more of college. That's where financial aid comes in.

Financial aid is possibly the most misunderstood topic of all when it comes to college preparation. Learning about and applying for aid is fairly straightforward – if time-consuming. Of course, if you find $500 or $5,000 to help defray your costs, it will be time well spent. By learning a few basic facts and following a few instructions you can make sure you're considered for every type of aid you qualify for.

Financial aid can be divided into two categories – merit-based and need-based. Merit-based aid is awarded based on your merit – what you have achieved, such as high ACT/SAT scores and GPA, leadership, and/or exceptional talent. It is usually awarded at the discretion of the college, company, or individual providing the money, usually in the form of a scholarship. Need-based aid is awarded based on your need – your ability to pay for college. It is often based on criteria, such as income level and family size, established by state and federal agencies. It comes mostly in the form of loans, grants, and work-study. Because you'll work on merit-based aid first chronologically, we'll cover that topic first.

Learning about and applying for aid is fairly straightforward – if time-consuming. Of course, if you find $500 or $5,000 to help defray your costs, it will be time well spent.

Merit-Based Aid: Scholarships

Applying for scholarships is the part of the college application process that requires the most work – by far. Students, you and your parents, or other family members, will spend a great deal of time investigating sources of funding, requesting applications, and filling them out.

SEARCHING FOR SCHOLARSHIPS

Before you students begin collecting information about scholarships, start a personal information file. You'll need this information when you start filling out applications. Make a list of all of the activities, clubs, and organizations you've been involved in since your freshman year of high school. Be sure to include any volunteer, church, or civic activities you have participated in. If you don't know what your cumulative grade point average and class rank are, find out by getting a copy of your transcript from your high school (your class rank may not be available until after your junior year, as many schools don't rank students until then). Include copies of any standardized test results. If you've ever written an essay about yourself or your goals, include a copy of that too.

Counselors often post new information about scholarships on web sites or bulletin boards, print it in newsletters, read it on the morning announcements, or send it out via an e-mail listserv.

Begin the process of finding scholarships during your junior year. Since most scholarships are awarded annually, being aware of what was awarded to the class ahead of you can pay big dividends. If you know students in the class ahead of you with similar scholarship potential to yours – similar grades or test scores, similar resume, similar field of study – ask them or their parents if they'd share their scholarship information with you when they're done. If you really want to be proactive, you can volunteer to help a senior locate scholarship information in exchange for receiving all the information when they're through. Although the contact person at an award-granting organization may change, deadlines, criteria, addresses, and the like will probably stay the

same or nearly the same. You can request information from that person at the beginning of your senior year and they'll send you the appropriate information and applications.

There are a number of other places to look for scholarship information as well. First and foremost is your high school counselor. (High school counselors are often willing to help you even after you've finished high school, but you won't be their first priority.) Counselors are generally the ones who receive information about new scholarships, so check with them periodically to see if there are any new scholarships you should be aware of. DO NOT EXPECT THEM TO TELL YOU ABOUT EACH ONE. Even if you have a very small graduating class, your counselor can't possibly remember what they've given to each of you. Often counselors post new information on web sites or bulletin boards, print it in newsletters, read it on the morning announcements or send it out via an e-mail listserv. So find out how yours does it –

again, if you're proactive, you could volunteer to help them post new information on a web page, type the newsletter, etc.

For scholarships specific to your chosen colleges, you should use the recruitment representative or admissions officer as a resource, as well as the school's web site. The recruiter should be able to let you know what you qualify for, but a little additional work could uncover additional funds. Universities are made up of many departments. Some may offer scholarships that are not as well publicized and may require separate applications. On rare occasions, departments may even find money to award to a student who impresses them to help encourage the student to choose their major. The bottom line is that you have to take the initiative and do a little hunting.

Other sources you should investigate are civic organizations in your community, churches, and the local library, where many books on scholarships are available. In addition, there is an enormous amount of information on scholarships available on the Internet. You can visit the homepage of your chosen schools and browse around. You can also use search engines to search for scholarships. One resource recommended by many people is the free FastWeb Scholarship Search located at **www. fastweb.com**.

On a rather touchy subject, I would like to make a comment regarding scholarship search companies. I neither endorse nor condemn outside search agencies that charge to locate scholarships for you. Some of these companies are absolutely reputable; some are not. If you are willing to do the work, you can usually find the same information for free.

APPLYING FOR SCHOLARSHIPS

There are so many scholarships available today, that there are too many different award criteria to list here. The most common criteria are:

- ▶ Grade point average.
- ▶ Rank in class.
- ▶ Standardized test scores.
- ▶ Extracurricular activities.
- ▶ Leadership.
- ▶ Community involvement.
- ▶ Special talents such as music and art.

Many colleges and organizations that award scholarships also take financial need into consideration.

Don't get the idea that you are expected to top out in every single area. You'll likely have one or two areas that are stronger than the others, which is to be expected. Awarding institutions look for well-rounded students, and regardless of the stated criteria for the award, a strong resume with varied experiences is almost always desirable.

You should expect to write an essay about yourself, your goals, or perhaps another subject. Many colleges require essays either as part of the admission application or the scholarship application, and private scholarships often require essays on various subjects. Some institutions will place a very high level of importance on the essay. Good writing can make a big difference. Some awarding institutions also state that clean, neat, accurate forms are an absolute must. In highly competitive situations, the decision whether or not to award often comes down to a misspelled word or something else very basic.

Most scholarships will have deadlines between November and March of your senior year. You should have all your resources gathered by November, sooner if you have an earlier deadline, and plan to have most of your applications completed before the New Year at the latest. Applications filled out at the last minute usually appear that way, so plan ahead. If there is a problem with an application you submit early, there will be time for you to fix it. If you are waiting on test scores to arrive in the mail, you should probably go ahead and send in the application, ensuring its arrival before the deadline, then contact the organization or college when your scores arrive. Given the choice between a late application with test scores included and an on-time application with test scores arriving a little later, I'd choose the latter.

ADDITIONAL SUGGESTIONS

▶ Always send thank-you notes to organizations and individuals that award the scholarships you receive.

▶ Your counselor is your best resource and friend in this process. Ask how you should go about keeping up with the latest information, without driving them nuts.

> **Applications filled out at the last minute usually appear that way, so plan ahead.**

▶ Do not hand-write applications. Use your computer to fill in digital forms, or a typewrite if it's an old fashioned paper form. Check spelling, and be sure to sign and date applications. Fill out all applicable spaces – incomplete applications may be eliminated from consideration.

Accepting a scholarship from a college is in no way, shape, or form a commitment to attend that school. Only when you show up for the first day of class are you truly committed. (What are they going to do, come to your house and drag you to school?) If a deadline to accept a scholarship arrives and you still haven't decided if you'll attend the school, but you are genuinely interested, accept the scholarship. You earned it, and you

it's a **BIG** world out there.
where do you wanna **GO?**

SNB offers student loans
to take you anywhere.

student loans. parent loans.
any college. any state.

apply online today with
your electronic signature.
www.banksnb.com/studentloans

SNB
Stillwater National Bank
Lender Code: 809081
800.678.GRAD

Member FDIC

should take whatever time you need to decide. Besides, the college will be able to find someone to take it if you later decide to decline. If you do decide to decline, notify the school promptly. In no way do I mean to encourage you to mislead a school. I do mean to encourage you to protect yourself and your interests.

Need-Based Aid

Need-based financial aid is intended to *help* you pay for college, not pay for it entirely. The federal government, which provides most need-based aid, has determined that the individual attending college and his or her immediate family have a responsibility to pay for a portion of college expenses.

FAFSA

The universal (or nearly universal) form that you and your family must use to provide schools and government agencies with financial information – annual income, savings, investments, number of college students in the family, etc. – is called the FAFSA, the acronym for Free Application for Federal Student Aid and pronounced faf-sa. Based on information you provide on the FAFSA, you will receive a notification that your information has been processed and that the schools you indicated as being of interest on the FAFSA now have access to that information. Based on that information, schools will determine your eligibility for federal financial aid. You should know that a school may not process your application any further until you have been admitted.

Parents, make it a point to complete your taxes as early as possible – preferably in January of your child's senior year.

Parents, make it a point to complete your taxes as early as possible – preferably in January of your child's senior year. This way, you'll also have all the information necessary to fill out the FAFSA so your child can be considered for aid as early as possible. Dragging your feet could cost your child some of the free money available to those who qualify and apply early. While some financial aid programs like the Pell Grant are entitlements – you get any money you qualify for regardless of when in the year's financial aid cycle you apply – most are not. Aid money in campus-based aid programs will run out, and those who apply earliest and who qualify get the money before it's all gone.

You must also be vigilant in responding to ANY request from the financial aid office at your chosen schools for additional information or verification of information. Not until your file is complete will your aid be processed.

Note that while you will need to have your tax forms at least partially completed, you do not currently have to submit your taxes to submit the FAFSA. Submit your FAFSA as soon as possible after January 1. Submit your tax forms to the IRS as soon as possible after that – increasingly schools use actual tax information to verify the FAFSA.

If you think the information you provided on the FAFSA doesn't appropriately reflect your situation, you can ask a school for special consideration of extenuating circumstances. While many people think their situation warrants special consideration, these instances usually involve a significant change in the student's or family's financial picture or a change that has occurred since the FAFSA was submitted. There will be procedures and guidelines that will determine if anything about your financial aid award can be changed, and how much. It is best not to expect a change based on extenuating circumstances, but you definitely won't get anything changed if you don't ask. If you feel your circumstances warrant special consideration, contact the financial aid office at the schools you are considering.

TYPES OF NEED-BASED AID

The main types of need-based financial aid are grants, work-study, and loans. Grants are like scholarships in that they are free money given to you to pay for college; unlike scholarships they are usually based on need, not merit. Work-study is student employment possibly related to your major, and either an on-campus job or community service, that is subsidized by the federal government (the federal subsidy makes it cheaper for the employer to hire a work-study student than someone not on work-study). Loans, as you would expect, are money borrowed to pay for college. Loans come from numerous sources, have different repayment terms, and even different borrowers – there are loans to students and loans to parents. Although some students and their families don't consider loans to be financial aid, since they're not free, that is exactly what they are. In fact, the vast majority of financial aid available for college students is made up of student loans and loans to parents.

A detailed discussion of specific financial aid types and amounts is more appropriate once you receive your award letter(s). At that time, the best source of information is that school's financial aid office.

It is important to remember – I'm talking mostly to students now – that financial aid is NOT intended to pay for car payments, credit card bills, cell phone bills, iPods, and other personal expenses. Schools prepare a budget annually that takes into consideration what it costs to live and go to school for the nine or ten-month academic year. Tuition, fees, room and board, travel, and incidentals are averaged from a sampling of what students actually spend. Financial aid is supposed to cover these costs; anything on top of them is your responsibility. Remember, when you're supported by financial aid, you may not be able to maintain the same lifestyle you've been accustomed to.

> **Apply for need-based aid early – as soon after January 1 as is possible. Aid money runs out before the number of qualified students runs out.**

REMINDERS FOR HIGH-SCHOOL SENIORS

▶ Apply for need-based aid early – as soon after January 1 as is possible. Aid money runs out before the number of qualified students runs out, so put yourself in the front of the line.

▶ If you are asked to provide more information or verify what you have submitted, respond immediately. It's likely your file will be in a holding pattern until your updates are received and your file processed.

▶ Do not send anything with your FAFSA or to your schools of choice that is not specifically requested. If you send additional documentation, schools may have to verify it, which can lengthen the process for you. The agency that processes the FAFSA will discard anything else they receive. You may later be required to submit additional documentation, but you may not.

▶ Students should fill out what they can on the FAFSA before passing it along to their parents for completion. There are a number of basic questions on the FAFSA like name, social security number, number of college students in the family, etc. If you fill out what you can, your parents will see that you are involved in the process and willing to do your share. That will make it easier on them, and they may be more willing to do what may not seem like fun at all.

▶ Notify the schools you plan to attend regarding all scholarships awarded to you. If you have scholarship assistance that they are not aware of, it could affect what you receive from that school. In addition, if a school finds out about a scholarship you didn't report to them, you might have to pay back some of your other aid.

▶ Once you've received an aid award letter for your freshman year, use that information to help you decide if you want or need to apply for aid in subsequent years of college. If you don't accept any of the aid you qualify for, your family financial picture stays relatively constant, and there are no additional students in college, you may decide not to reapply. However, if something changes, you should go back and apply at that time.

REMINDERS FOR STUDENTS IN COLLEGE

▶ Don't forget to re-apply each year. The form for re-applying is slightly different from the original FAFSA, but is still available at **www.fafsa.ed.gov**.

▶ Don't drop or add classes without finding out whether and how it will affect your financial aid. Dropping too many courses too often can cause you to lose your aid.

▶ Keep your physical address and e-mail address current with your college and the financial aid office. Colleges will likely use the last address you gave them to send letters to. If you're a senior in college and your parents moved last year, or the school still lists your address as the dorm you lived in freshman year, they won't be able to get in touch with you if there is a problem or they need more information.

▶ Know that there are emergency and/or short-term loans available for when the unexpected happens. You are likely to receive these loans only if you will have the ability to repay them soon. Special forms and requirements will likely apply.

> **Financial aid is NOT intended to pay for car payments, credit card bills, cellphone bills, iPods, and other personal expenses.**

Money at School

Just as you discussed money during the application process, you should talk again before you pack up the car and head to school – and as needed after that. Questions to answer include:

▶ Who has control of and/or access to what bank accounts?

▶ Should accounts stay at the bank at home or be moved to a bank in the college town?

▶ Should funds be doled out at the beginning of the

school year? Once a semester? Monthly? Or on some other schedule?

▶ How much will be doled out?

▶ Students, are you allowed or required to get a job? Will the answer to this question change after your freshman year?

▶ Who pays for what?

▶ Should you have a credit card? A debit card? An ATM card?

▶ Parents, is there any possibility you'll send more money once the agreed-on amount is exhausted?

SPENDING MONEY

When I was a university recruiter, parents often asked how much spending-money a college student needs on a weekly or monthly basis. My first answer was always that your child will "need" as much as you give them. After all, the college experience usually includes an unlimited supply of clothing stores, concerts, sporting events, road trips (yes, your child will leave school and drive someplace other than home), pizza, and MP3s.

If students are paying for the extras out of their own pocket or out of a finite amount of cash, they'll have to prioritize and purchase what is most important to them. The catch here is that you have to be the bad guy when the kids come begging for more. College is a great time and place for your child to start understanding the value of money and the skills involved in managing it. It's better for students to mess up their finances during college, while parents are still involved, than once they're out in the real world and dealing with insurance, a mortgage, or the electric bill.

The real answer to the spending-money question is different for each student and family. Different people define spending money differently, and different families decide who pays for what differently. The bottom line is that they'll need more money during the first couple of weeks of school. Students, you should keep close track of what you spend in those first weeks. Only after that will you and your parents really know how much is appropriate. Then you can have a frank discussion about how much you need and how much you're getting.

The final meeting on college finances should take place a couple of weeks into school and should include setting rules for how and when you parents will make adjustments to the plan. After you see how much your student has spent and where, you can reconnect about who pays for what. Regardless of what you decide, realize that there are far more expenses at the beginning of the semester, particularly at the very beginning of school, so plan to have more cash available then.

If you decide a credit card is appropriate for your child, allow and, if necessary, help your child get ONE card – no more. Students, you should use the card once to purchase something that can be paid off over several months and, after that, use it only for emergencies. By emergencies I mean things like an emergency room visit or towing the car when it breaks down in the middle of the night. Sweaters, dates, and iPods usually don't constitute emergencies. The card should be in the student's name, with parents as co-signers if necessary. Having and using the credit card helps young people establish a credit history so they can finance a car or home or furniture to furnish that first apartment when they graduate. Without a credit history, it will be more difficult to do all of these things.

College is a great time and place for your child to start understanding the value of money and the skills involved in managing it.

Parents, be sure also to warn your child about all the credit card companies that prey – yes, that's the right word – on naïve college students. Some companies offer nice enticements to sign up for cards with high credit limits so they're attractive to college students, who won't think twice (or maybe even once) about the 18 or 21 percent interest rate. These companies bank on the fact that students won't make the right choices, will spend too much, and will get bailed out by their parents.

> **Parents, be sure to warn your child about all the credit card companies that prey on naïve college students.**

Help your child set up a budget and turn over management of their finances to an increasing degree as their experience and success grows. It's probably best for you to be a little more involved at the beginning and reduce your involvement as time goes on.

If at all possible, I suggest that first-semester freshmen not be required to work. Freshmen have a tough enough time getting used to college life and studying without the added time commitment of a job. Once they've gotten their feet under them they'll be better prepared to manage outside employment.

Making the Transition to College

Graduating from high school and moving on to the next stage of life is a rite of passage that most of you will experience. While college is a bit more protected than the world of full-time work, it is still a major change from the high school environment most of you are accustomed to. Those of you who are best prepared and most knowledgeable about what's to come are likely to be most successful. The more you think about college, read about college, spend time on college campuses, and talk to people about college, the more you'll know what to expect and the better prepared you'll be.

To prepare for the move from high school to college, you must first know what the differences are. Many of the differences can be divided into two categories – academic and social.

Much of the difficulty students experience transitioning from high school to college involves newfound freedoms and the choices these freedoms entail.

Academic differences

Academic differences are probably more commonly discussed, like when a senior English teacher says, "Those are the kind of mistakes that will really cost you in college." Here are some of the bigger ones:

▶ Classes are generally larger – sometimes with as many as a few hundred students in a single class. In big lecture classes, professors are less likely to know who you are.

▶ Classes are more challenging and require more outside reading and studying. In high school, it isn't uncommon for students to do well just because of natural intelligence. In college, even the smartest have to study to do well.

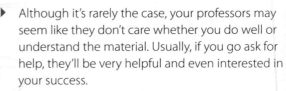

- Although it's rarely the case, your professors may seem like they don't care whether you do well or understand the material. Usually, if you go ask for help, they'll be very helpful and even interested in your success.

- Professors may not regularly remind you about upcoming assignments, papers, quizzes, or tests. Often they'll hand out a complete syllabus on the first day and expect you to remember due dates on your own.

- Academic dishonesty, though not a very positive topic, is a growing problem on college campuses. Basically, academic dishonesty is any attempt to gain academic credit for something that isn't originally yours, e.g., turning in someone else's work as your own, not quoting or citing information you borrow from sources, copying other students' work, using cheating devices (cheat sheets, 2-way radios, cell phone calculators, text messaging answers to or from another student, etc.), or supplying inappropriate help to someone else. In high school these things were obviously wrong, but the penalties weren't that harsh. In college the punishments for these offenses can range from an F for that assignment or test to an F for the course, academic suspension, or expulsion from school.

- Not everyone who teaches a class is a professor. College teachers can be divided into two main categories – professors and instructors – with several divisions in each category. The categories and divisions indicate differing degrees of expertise, experience, and academic achievement. Starting from the highest ranking, you'll most likely study with:

  - ▶▶ Full professors. They have the most experience teaching, have advanced degrees in their field, have done years of research, and have a permanent status at their school called tenure. They are often considered experts in their field, and many have written one or

more books, chapters in books, or research articles. They may also be department heads, deans, or even the university president. Some have prestigious titles indicating prominence within their field, e.g., chairs or professorships named after university donors, foundations or corporations – Dr. Frederick S. Smith, Professor and Dupont Chair, Department of Chemistry.

▶▶ Associate professors. They have the same education as professors but have slightly less experience in teaching and research. They have tenure but are in the process of attaining the experience and prestige of full professors.

▶▶ Assistant professors. They have the same education as associate and full professors, but they are building their resume with research, teaching, and outside work in an attempt to earn tenure.

▶▶ Graduate assistants (GAs) and teaching assistants (TAs). These are graduate students pursuing their masters or doctoral degrees.

Most often, they are helping a professor. In some departments, GAs and TAs may be alone teaching a class, though usually under the supervision of a professor. Because GAs and TAs are students, many undergraduates feel they relate better to them than professors.

▶▶ Instructors and lecturers. They have education and/or experience that qualifies them to teach the subject, but their position is less permanent, usually semester-to-semester or year-to-year, or they may be teaching part-time, perhaps in addition to another job – e.g., a practicing lawyer who teaches a business law course.

So, you might ask, what do I call all these people? Usually, they'll identify themselves on the first day of class. Professors might say, "I'm Professor So-and-so," or "I'm Doctor Such-and-such." Teaching assistants or instructors might say, "I'm Ms. Jones," or "I'm Rebecca." Call them whatever they call themselves. (Note also that full, associate, and assistant professors are all called "professor" if they use that title rather than "doctor.")

Social differences

Every decision you make has repercussions. Good decisions tend to put you in a position to get what you want.

While the academic differences between high school and college may seem to be the most important, I think the social differences will be more likely to give you trouble. By social, I don't just mean the parties or meeting new people, although that's part of it. I mean how you relate to and handle the new people, situations, and environments you'll find yourself in.

Much of the difficulty students experience transitioning from high school to college involves newfound freedoms and the choices these freedoms entail. In high school your freedom was probably fairly limited, and numerous people influenced your decisions. In college, all of that will change. You'll be free to do most anything you want, the people around you will be new, and they are likely to exert less direct influence over you. You'll be managing your own life and making your own decisions. You'll also be living with the consequences of the decisions you make.

You will be in charge! You will be the one choosing when to go to bed, when to wake up, whether or not you go to class, what you do and don't do, who you associate with, how you dress, whether or not you pay your bills on time, if you drink alcohol and how much, if and when you balance your checkbook and how you manage your money, whether or not you clean your room, etc. These and many other choices will have different consequences, depending on how you handle them.

Know yourself and act accordingly.

Staying up extremely late only once in a while will affect your grades much less than staying up late so often that you miss class on regular basis. Similarly, drinking alcohol in moderation only occasionally won't affect you as much as drinking heavily three or four times a week. Every decision you make will have repercussions. Good decisions tend to put you in a position to get what you want – good grades, stable finances, good health, etc. – while bad ones often cause problems – bad grades, money problems, angry parents.

You should plan for two main things when you go to college: bad influences and more choices than you thought you'd ever have to make. Hopefully you'll have mostly good influences and make mostly the right choices, but if you prepare for the worst, you'll be ready for whatever you get.

Although these differences can be significant, there are a couple of important similarities that can help you deal with the rough spots. First, you are the same person. If you were successful enough in high school to be admitted to college, the same intelligence, hard work, and dedication will serve you well in college – academically and socially. Second, there is lots of support available if you need it. From academic help to career guidance to personal counseling and beyond, virtually anything you could possibly want or need is available in college. You just have to seek it out.

Helpful hints

The following are a few ideas that I think will help you prepare for the differences between high school and college.

▶ Take high school seriously. Developing good study habits early will help in college.

▶ Inform yourself. Use this book as a stepping stone to further reading about college life, financial aid, personal growth, etc.

▶ Talk to people in college and others your age about the transition.

▶ Visit friends at college, and go to college events as frequently as possible.

▶ Spend a good deal of time on your college's web site. It will give you an idea of what's important there and what students are doing.

▶ Know that all your actions will have repercussions. Think ahead of time about decisions you know you'll have to make – drinking and drugs, missing class, sex, etc. Don't be surprised if some of the choices you make in college are different than they were in high school.

▶ Know yourself and act accordingly. If you procrastinate, plan to stay home right before tests – no going out, no intramural games – or make yourself get started early. If you know you're not fully functional early in the morning, don't sign up for early classes. Don't set yourself up for failure.

What to Bring to College

It's an exciting day, and maybe a little sad, packing the stuff in your room at home to take to your new home at college. As simple as moving might seem, it can be quite a challenging process. In campus residences and fraternity/sorority houses, I've seen many rooms overflowing with junk that will never be used, and conversely students who have had to borrow everything from roommates or new neighbors. Avoid either extreme, and aim somewhere in the middle. Space is usually at a premium, so efficiency is the goal.

So What Should I Bring?

The first thing you should do is contact your roommate and coordinate what each of you will bring. There's not much point to having two refrigerators and no TV or, worse still, two of everything!

Here is a list of things that will likely come in handy during the year. Not all of them are a must, but the list may include some you hadn't thought of.

Fashion Faux Pas: Leave the high school memorabilia at home. Yes, even the letter jacket.

- ✔ Television.
- ✔ DVD player.
- ✔ Microwave.
- ✔ Refrigerator or a micro-fridge combo unit.
- ✔ Cell phone with good service/coverage where your college is.
- ✔ Digital camera to capture all your new friends and fun.
- ✔ iPod or MP3 player, and stereo with a docking station.
- ✔ Computer, preferably a laptop, with printer and other necessary peripherals.

- Three-prong extension cords.
- Power strip/surge protector.
- Sports equipment – football, volleyball, basketball, rackets, shoes, etc.
- Desk lamp.
- Alarm clock (maybe two).
- Laundry bag or basket.
- Laundry soap.
- Stain remover.
- Knowledge of how to do laundry or money to pay someone to do it.
- One or more rolls of quarters for laundry, the Coke machine, tolls, etc.
- Sewing kit with needles and thread, safety pins, two-sided tape, etc.
- Eating utensils, preferably plastic.
- Cups and plates, also plastic or Styrofoam – washing dishes in a community bathroom isn't fun.
- Bedding and one or more good blankets because it can get cold in campus housing.
- Anything to decorate your room and make you feel at home.
- Iron and small ironing board.
- PDA/organizer/planner.
- Backpack.
- College clothes, and you might leave the high school t-shirts and letter jackets at home.
- Bike and a good bike lock.
- Fan because campus housing may have poor air circulation.
- Bath towels, soap, robe, etc.
- Personal hygiene items – toothpaste, deodorant, etc.
- Shower shoes, flip flops, or Crocs.
- Shower caddy for toiletries.
- Small can-opener and bottle opener.

- First aid kit including Band-aids, antibiotic ointment, ace bandage, etc.
- Tylenol or other pain reliever.
- Umbrella.
- Raincoat.
- Rain shoes/boots.
- Pictures of family, friends, and pets.
- Your insurance card and health insurance information.
- Phonebook from your hometown so you can call and order flowers for your Mom on her birthday.
- Swimsuit(s).
- Workout/sports clothes.
- Dress clothes – guys, this means at least a blazer and one or more ties.
- Grubby clothes – who knows if you'll volunteer to go clean up along the highway or paint someone's house, or need to play mud football.
- Confidence.
- Positive attitude.

Okay, So What Should I Leave at Home?

- ⊘ Pets – fish are marginally okay, except piranhas.
- ⊘ High school memorabilia and letter jackets.
- ⊘ Full size refrigerator – rooms are only so big.
- ⊘ Firearms, even if you hunt or shoot for sport – most campuses don't allow guns, and even if you have an off-campus apartment, gun security won't be as good as back home.
- ⊘ Expensive clothing and jewelry – this is the real world, theft does occur.
- ⊘ Out-of-season clothes – your closet is only so big. If you live far from your school, bring a light jacket and some long sleeve shirts for unexpected weather changes and for cold buildings. Get next season's clothes when you go home.

It might be best to leave your ol' pal Einstein at home.

Sharpening Your Study Skills

10

Perhaps the most important skill needed for success in college is the ability to study effectively. Each person comes to college with his or her own strengths, weaknesses, study experience, intellectual ability, and will to work hard. Different people need help with different aspects of studying.

A variety of skills and strategies are necessary for different types of classes, different professors and teaching styles, and, most importantly, different students. It's important for you to figure out and practice your personal style of studying. While the best way to discover what does and doesn't work is to try different things, your grades probably can't stand too many errors. The trick is to figure out what works quickly – or at least eliminate the things that don't. The better and more efficiently you study, the less time school work will take, and the more time you'll have for other things.

The better and more efficiently you study, the less time schoolwork will take, and the more time you'll have for other things.

As any reporter can tell you, there are six important questions to answer when investigating any topic – the five W's – who, what, when, where, why – plus the all important how. Answer these questions regarding your study habits and you'll be on the path to greater success.

Who To Study With

When it comes to "who," the first question you need to answer here is whether you can study with other people at all. While most students would agree that studying with others is useful, you may or may not be productive in that situation. Whether you're studying the same subject with others or just studying at the same time, you have to be committed to studying and not socializing or goofing off.

Assuming you've determined that you can study with others, the best thing you can do for yourself is study with a student who is good in the subject, especially someone who's knowledgeable about the things you're not, or someone who looks at things from a different perspective. Most likely, you'll both find the different points of view helpful.

Studying with a significant other can be fun, but the temptation to take "make-out" breaks will be a constant threat to your study time. You need to be able to maintain focus on studying course material and not your study partner.

What To Study

The answer might seem obvious, but you'd be surprised by how many students do poorly in a class or in college because they either studied the wrong material or didn't know what to study. Some professors test exclusively out of the textbook and treat their lectures as simply additional information. Some do the exact opposite. Some test your knowledge of optional texts or study guides. It's important to know whether specific details or broad concepts are what the professor is looking for. Does he ask trick questions? Does she expect you to know obscure facts? On papers or written assignments, is inclusion of all the correct facts important, or do grammar, spelling, and punctuation count most?

Professors have different styles and methods of grading, so it's very important to find out what they want – and quickly. By talking to students who have had your professors before, you'll know what to expect. It's also a very good idea to talk with your professors and graduate/teaching assistants to find out straight from them. I've even heard of professors who will give you extra information or access to non-public resources, but only if you go talk with them.

When To Study

The best time to study is ahead of time and as your class goes along – not at the last minute. The bottom line is the amount you study for a class is completely within your control – even if problems come up at the last minute. If you study well ahead of when something is due or a test is to be given, things that just come up have less effect on your grade. In addition, if you study as you go along in a class it will make more sense to you, you will get more out of the lectures, and you won't need to do as much cramming at the last minute.

As for specifically when you should study, the most common time college students study is at night. While that's probably when you'll do most of your studying, utilizing other times of the day can really pay off. If you think about it, most of what you'll want to do socially – dates, hanging out with friends – will be at night. If night is the only time you study, you'll have to decide whether you'll study or go out. To avoid having to make the choice, consider other options. In other words, don't make study time compete with fun time. Study first and you'll be able to go have fun when you want.

You can't always schedule your classes back-to-back, so you may have one or two hours or more between some of your classes. Depending on how close you live and where your job is, if you have one, you may not have time to go home or work during that break. Often, when students live close enough to go back to their room between classes, the time is spent napping, watching television, playing video or computer games, or Facebooking. While there may not be enough time

TIP

Study first and you'll be able to have fun when you want.

to read an entire chapter or start work on a paper, there should be time to review class notes, browse a chapter or two, outline a paper, write down questions to ask your professor, etc.

Where To Study

Like the other questions, where you study is a very individual thing. While it's probably most common for people to study where they live, I'd suggest someplace else. If possible, don't study where you eat, sleep, or have fun. That only makes it easier and more likely you'll take a break or quit studying to do one of those other things. Try to find a place of your own to study away from where you live.

Colleges have tons of different kinds of places to choose from, depending on your needs. Try out a few different locations and see what you like and where you get your work done. Between classes one day, take a stroll through the library and check out the possibilities. Do the same in the student union and other buildings that

are open late. You'll see other students tucked into little nooks and crannies all over the place. Some people like tables in a cafeteria-type area with lots of activity going on around them. Some need solitude and a comfortable chair. Others find cubicle-type study areas in the library or residence halls helpful. Still others need to spread all their books out on a table in front of them and don't care where it's located. The point is to figure out what works for you. Find a place or two that meet your needs and go there to study. If you get hungry when studying, take some food or drink with you. You want to be able to go there, get studying done very efficiently, and go home. It's also best if you can turn your cell phone off. Whoever is calling can probably wait an hour or two to talk to you.

Try out a few different study locations and see what you like and where you get your work done.

Why Study

Some people study hard to earn good grades, while others study to learn the material (there is a difference!). Others study only enough to earn a specific grade or to stay in school or maintain membership in some organization. Some are only in college because it is expected of them, rather than because they want to be. It's common for some to have different standards for different classes. For example, some students may study to learn in classes specific to their major but just to get by in general education classes.

As long as you know why you're doing what you're doing, it will be easier to plan your studying appropriately.

How To Study

The answer to the "how" question might just be why you started reading this chapter – to get to the practical nuts and bolts of getting your work done. Here are a few lists of strategies and ideas that many students have found useful in preparing for college classes. Because there are probably as many ways to study as there are students studying, the list shouldn't be considered all-inclusive. However, there should be enough ideas for anyone to find some suggestions helpful. They are presented in various categories and in what I believe is the order you're most likely to use them.

Classes

- Go to class every day, especially just before holidays or big on-campus events – those are popular times for other students to miss class and for professors to give extra credit or pop quizzes.
- Meet your professors.
- Sit in the same place every class period. This makes it easy for the professor to notice you're there.
- Sit at or near the front of the class.
- Ask questions and participate in class discussions. If you're uncomfortable doing that, it's even more important for you to visit your professors' office and talk with them.
- Don't read the paper or sleep during class – you'd be surprised, but people actually do this. Professors get offended and you don't want them to remember you for that.
- If you have to miss class, try to notify your professor ahead of time and try to get notes from a classmate. When you return, contact the professor again to discuss what you missed, not IF you missed anything.
- Remember, whatever subject you're studying, the professor has dedicated ten years or more of his or her life to studying and teaching the subject. Even if you hate the subject, don't let on. To your professor, it's the most intellectually stimulating subject there is.

Note-Taking

▶ Develop your own style – everyone takes notes differently.

▶ Use abbreviations and feel free to make up your own – w/ for "with," b/c for "because," etc. In your notes, pretend you're IM-ing or texting.

▶ Write down words, phrases, or ideas repeated in lecture.

▶ Don't write everything down.

▶ Leave room in your notes to add your own thoughts later on. Some people make extra wide margins on one side of the paper so they can add notes about their notes later on. Some leave room by skipping every other line.

▶ Consider trading notes with someone else so you will see what he or she thought was important.

▶ Take notes in outline form or add marks later – numbers, letters, bullets – indicating levels of importance or organization of concepts

▶ Rewrite your notes after class is over.

▶ Review your notes within one day of taking them.

▶ Ask the professor about topics you didn't understand or have incomplete notes on.

▶ Use paper, pens, and hi-lighters as needed – they're not that expensive.

Go to class every day, especially just before holidays or big on-campus events.

▶ Ask professors if they have notes you can look at to see if you are getting the main points.

▶ Take the textbook to class and write notes in it – this is particularly useful if the professor uses the book a great deal. Feel free to mark it up however you want; it belongs to you. Use color-coded pens, hi-lighters, and underlining for different types of information. E.g., material hi-lighted in pink could be an essay question, words circled w/ red pen are definitely vocabulary words on the test, etc.

▶ Make drawings, maps, graphs as necessary.

▶ Place stars next to important information.

▶ Use post-it notes or tabs to mark important information in the book.

Writing Papers

▶ Use spell check. Then check on your own for the wrong word spelled correctly (there, their, they're, etc.)

▶ Have someone else read your paper, and don't be upset when they give you suggestions – you don't have to use them if you don't want.

▶ Write a draft, and let some time pass (days if possible) before you rewrite it. You'll find mistakes, think of better ways of saying the same thing, and make it a better paper.

▶ Make use of campus resources such as a writing lab, or have a junior or senior in the same major edit your work.

▶ Don't be hardheaded. If the way you wrote papers in high school earned you A's, but it now earns you C's, change to accommodate what your college professor wants.

Studying

▶ Use a planner/calendar to write down everything you will be graded on, then write down all the non-academic activities and events you'll be involved in, so you can plan your studying around the rest of your life. Schedule time to study as well as time to have fun.

▶ Study early, often, and not for long periods of time (more than a couple of hours) without a break.

▶ Buy new or slightly used textbooks – that don't already have notes or hi-lighting in them – you never know how smart or how good a student the previous owner was.

▶ Read textbooks, study guides, notes and any other resources suggested by your professor.

▶ Study with classmates and help each other, as long as you'll actually study.

▶ Eliminate distractions – if you sing along with the radio, turn it off; if you're bothered by the noise of your roommates, go somewhere quiet, etc.

▶ Be prepared to study when you sit down to study. Have supplies ready, food and drink if you'll need it, and a clear mind.

▶ Focus on the quality of your study, not just how long you study.

▶ Be aware of when you write best, when you read best, when you study best. Do those things then.

▶ Always carry something you could take out and study for 10, 15, or 30 minutes. A professor might be late to class, your bus could be late, or your friend might not show up on time.

Consider trading notes with someone else so you will see what he or she thought was important.

▶ Check the library and your professors' web pages for resources or other help they make available.

▶ Don't forget to read and review tables, charts, graphs, and images in the textbook or study guide.

▶ When you think you know questions that will be on the test, especially essay questions, write out answers or all you know about the topic ahead of time.

▶ Make and use flashcards.

▶ Rewrite and restate aloud what you are studying. Writing and saying information are useful tools in learning. They use your brain differently and make it easier to be retained.

Studying in Groups

▶ Be selective about the people you study with – make sure YOU'LL benefit.

▶ Talk to everyone about how they study, what they think will be on the test, and what format they think the professor looks for. Get more perspectives on the material.

▶ Divide material between group members and make it each person's responsibility to teach everyone else.

Test-Taking

▶ Know when tests are scheduled and record them in your calendar/organizer.

▶ Know what format tests will be in – multiple choice, matching, essay, etc.

▶ Ask your professor ahead of time any questions you have about the test.

▶ Utilize test files maintained by residence halls or fraternities/sororities. This isn't cheating as long as the materials were secured through legitimate means. It just gives you an idea what that professor has asked in the past, and how they ask things.

▶ Talk to students who have taken that class or professor previously, the more recently the better.

▶ Relax and don't let tests ruin your life. Prepare and study; be concerned about knowing the material, but don't stress about it. Stress can hurt your performance and keep you from showing what you know.

▶ Use all resources available to you – books, notes, study guides, other people, the professor, etc.

▶ Get as much sleep as possible right before the test, and eat right.

▶ If possible, ask for help from the professor before the test, not after.

▶ On essays, when time is running out and you don't have enough time to finish, write down as many facts as you know about the subject without

Be selective about the people you study with – make sure YOU'LL benefit.

regard for grammar, spelling, etc. It will show the professor what you knew but didn't have time to write, and it could help your grade.

▶ Guess rather than leaving things blank.

▶ Be sure to answer all parts of each question.

▶ Answer the easy questions first.

▶ If allowed to use notes or the book during tests, know where things are, even if you don't know everything about them, and label things. If you're allowed to use a cheat sheet, write extremely small and use both sides of the paper.

Extra Strategies For Success

▶ Be smart about studying. Prioritize material and time. Study what you know will be on the test and likely worth the most in terms of your grade.

▶ Ask for help at the first sign you need it; don't wait till right before the test or even after it.

▶ Make school your first priority, at least when you're studying.

▶ When you read and re-read something and nothing sinks in, you are likely thinking about something else. Do something about it. Call the person you are thinking about, resolve whatever is unresolved, pay the bill you are worried about, tell your folks your grades might be lower than you'd like, etc. Deal with whatever is bothering you, and then concentrate on studying.

▶ Always know where your grade in each class stands. If a professor tells you you're doing fine or you'll be okay, clarify what "fine" or "okay" means.

▶ Get involved in your education. You are in charge of making it happen. Make yourself care about "boring" subjects, etc.

▶ Read material before it's covered in class. Then the lecture will tell you what's important and add the professor's perspective to the material.

▶ Stay awake:

   ▶▶ Study when you are wide-awake.

   ▶▶ Don't study and sleep in the same location, especially not in bed.

   ▶▶ Study in a fully lit room.

   ▶▶ Chew gum, eat candy, or eat sunflower seeds (my personal favorite) to help stay awake when you're sleepy.

   ▶▶ Be careful with caffeine. While it may pick you up for a time, you will likely experience a letdown once it wears off. You may also experience poor concentration while it's in your system.

   ▶▶ Don't use any of the commercially available products aimed at keeping you awake.

   ▶▶ Don't even consider using drugs, legal or not, to keep you awake. Any benefits are short term and aren't worth the consequences.

   ▶▶ If you're tired, get up and walk around while reading your notes.

Time Management

Time management is one of the most important skills necessary for success as a college student. The change from the structured, predictable world of high school to the unstructured, less predictable world of college is often difficult. The things that created the structure in your life, like school, work, family, church, and friends, are probably gone. Since you are the only constant, you have to take control of your life and your time.

Those who haven't mastered the art of time management commonly complain that there isn't enough time in the day. The sooner you learn to manage your time, the easier your time will be. When students don't have a set of priorities or the ability to make the right choices – do I go out or do I study? – they often make poor decisions. For many first starting out in college, the priority is to do everything they weren't allowed to do at home or meet as many members of the opposite sex as possible. Usually, these students don't do particularly well in school and have to reassess what is important. They might even have to move back home and work for a semester or two because of poor academic performance. Hopefully, you'll figure out how to set and keep your priorities before you make any bad grades or create problems for yourself .

You can fit more in your day if you open your mind to finding just when you might do it.

Filling Your Day

Students often think they are "maxed out" and don't have enough time to do what they need to do. To impress upon students that they have more time than they think they do, I use the following example.

By determining the order of your personal priorities, you'll find that individual tasks or goals will begin to order themselves.

A speaker stands at the front of a freshman orientation class. The speaker holds up a large, empty glass pickle jar, the kind you find next to the cash register at convenience stores. He tells the audience to imagine the jar is a day in their lives. He then begins to place tennis balls in the jar, saying that each ball represents something they do during the day, like studying, going to class, working, sleeping, etc. He places the last ball in the jar, leaving just enough room to put on the lid and tighten it down. He asks, "Is your day full?" In unison, the class answers "YES!" He replies, "NO, it isn't. There's plenty of room left in there." He proceeds to pull out a large bag of marbles from beneath the table, and one by one, he puts the marbles in the "full" jar. When he's done, he asks again if it's full. Some say "yes," while some just don't answer. He helps them out, with "NO, it's not full." He pulls out a large box of BBs and pours its contents into the "full" jar, stopping once to shake the BBs down in the jar. "Is it full?" Starting to catch on, a couple in the class seem to ask "NO?" "NO!" he says, pulling out a bag of sand. Filling the jar, he asks the same question again, "Is it full?" Some answer "Yes" thinking his exhibition is over. Others just keep quiet, wondering if he's done. "NO" he says. What does he pull out this time? A pitcher of water! After pouring it in the jar, he tells the class "It's full now!"

The lesson he wants the students to understand is that they can fit a lot more into their day than they might initially think – they just have to know how to make it fit. You too can fit more into your day if you open your mind to finding just when you might do it.

Full-Time Job

One way you can have the right frame of mind about school is to treat it as if it's your full-time job. Preparing for class, going to class, studying, talking to professors, networking, and educating yourself about your degree field are all parts of the job. It's difficult getting used to a full-time job where you make all the decisions and your work schedule is completely under your control, but if you can overcome that obstacle, you stand a good chance of being successful. As I mentioned before, it's a question of priorities.

Priorities

I would never tell anyone that school should be their first priority. For some, school will be No. 1, but for many, faith or family or something else will rank higher. Regardless, school must be a very high priority. By determining the order of your personal priorities, you'll find that individual tasks or goals will begin to order themselves. By determining which seemingly competing activities are your higher priorities, your decision is much easier to make. Setting and keeping priorities provides a framework you can use to help you decide what to do and when to do it.

Once your priorities are set, you have to keep them. That means taking action that leads to the achievement of your stated goals and choosing to do what you should do, rather than what you want to do. Early in college, students often struggle with priorities, sometimes choosing to participate in too many social or leadership activities or even counterproductive activities at the expense of academic or personal goals. Much of that is short-lived and can be overcome once freedom isn't so new. Some students struggle with connecting their choices with their priorities, some don't grow up as fast as others, and still others don't ever make the academic part of college a priority. As I mentioned, I don't think school has to be everyone's top priority, and I don't think it has to be anybody's top priority all the time. For example, a political science major might run for student government president. During the campaign and the time in office, it's very likely that grades in general or in certain classes might not be as important as they would be otherwise. It would be difficult to fault them for that decision, given the value of a campus-wide campaign in preparation for future campaigns.

Get Organized

OK, so you've got your priorities straight, and you're committed to keeping them and making the right choices. Now what? It's time to get organized! You have to know what's coming up and plan for it. That means keeping track of everything, and that means using an organizer. Organizers come in many shapes and sizes, but I suggest something you can always have with you, like a calendar/planner book or a PDA or other hand-held device.

The first thing you do with your organizer is fill it up. List every grade or assignment in each of your classes, and its deadline. Enter all the activities you'll be involved in and the events and meetings you'll be attending. Once you know what you have to do and when, then you can go through and block off time to write papers, study for tests, and otherwise arrange your time to support your academic efforts.

For example, if you have a quiz coming up, you may only need to block off an hour or two the night before to be ready for it. If you have a test, however, you'll need to set aside a couple of hours every night for a week, plus maybe some time during the day to meet with your professor, and most of the evening before the test for that test alone. Or you might start working on a paper a week early, spend a few hours writing your first draft, then not work on it again for a couple of days, then pick it up again, re-write it, have somebody edit it a few nights before it's due, then need only an hour or so to fine tune it before handing it in.

Use an organizer you can always carry with you, like a calendar/ planner book or a PDA or other hand-held device.

The most important thing, however, is using your organizer! Keep it with you all the time so you'll be able to check what's coming up next and make changes as necessary. That way when that attractive person you've been hoping to meet sits down next to you in class and asks if you'd like to go and get a latte sometime, you can look and see that you have several things due on Wednesday, and that Thursday might be a good time to go.

Just because you have put together a plan and are organized, doesn't mean you can't be flexible. Just remember to replace time you take away for another purpose. If you run into an old friend and want to chat during a time when you were planning to study, go ahead. Just remember to make up the study time by shortening a couple of study breaks, eating lunch more quickly than usual, or staying up a little later that night. You can use your organizer to know when you're free to go out with friends or meet with a professor. Having most everything written down, you'll be much less likely to forget something.

As you learn to organize your to do's, you'll get a real feeling of satisfaction when you cross things off your list.

To Do Lists

Another thing you can use your organizer for is keeping track of your to do lists. Almost without exception, paper organizers/calendars provide space on the page and digital organizers include task list functions. As you learn to organize your to do's, you'll get a real feeling of satisfaction when you cross things off your list. When you reach the end of a day, week, or month and have an item or two that still need to be completed, simply turn the page and put them at the top of the next to do list. If you seem to continually move the same item from list to list, you probably need to think about why you're putting it off. Do you need help to accomplish the task? Are you just not finished yet? Is it really that important to you?

Timing

One thing that is a very important component of time management is something you may have to make yourself do – being aware of and placing a high value on time. That can mean anything from being on time to class, meetings, or appointments, to not over-sleeping. So use a watch, or at least the clock on your cell phone, and get a good alarm clock – or two if it takes a lot to wake you up! Being late sends the message that you had something more important that you were doing, and often makes it appear you think your time is more valuable than others'. It shows a lack of respect. Your boss is going to expect you to be on time when you get out of college, you don't want to offend a professor who

holds your grade in her hand, and you better show respect to your boyfriend or girlfriend or you'll be looking for a new one. Respect your time and the time of others.

A Little More

▶ Don't over-commit or over-extend. Resist the temptation to always say yes when asked to help out with something. Effective time managers are more likely to do a few things very well than lots of things not as well. Make time for the commitments that are important to you.

▶ When conflicts arise, check your priorities. Do what's most important first, not what's easiest or most fun. You'll usually feel better having completed the more important task, and then have a clear conscience when doing the easy, fun stuff.

▶ Use time during the day, between classes, when there's little else going on. You can bet that all the fun stuff – and the temptation to participate – will happen at night, whether it's intramural sports, movies, friends going out, or parties. If you've studied or done your to do's during the day, you'll be able to go out and not worry that you should be doing something else..

Thoughts for Parents

12

During the years when your child finds the right college and finally leaves the nest, the most important thing you will be helping them do is develop personal responsibility. While academic and financial responsibility are probably the two most obvious areas they will develop, they'll also need your counsel on myriad other topics. If you engage them in friendly conversation, ask open-ended questions, and listen – really listen – you will learn what your child thinks about all the new things going on. And believe me, you'll have opportunities to offer input. These are the times you'll be able to help them make the right decisions and be reassured they know the right way to make those decisions.

A word of warning. Your life will change as well. You might experience "empty nest syndrome" as you deal with the absence of a major part of your life. If you do, my advice would be – get busy! New activities can help fill your time and change your perspective. Bear in mind, your child doesn't need to be worrying about you. Don't allow family situations back home to burden them unduly. They need space and freedom to grow and thrive.

Get Involved

A good way to smooth your own transition is to take pride in your child's college. Buy a shirt, hat, or bumper sticker – or all three – that shouts to the world that your child attends this university or is a member of that organization.

Most schools also offer parents ways to participate actively. Join the college's parents' organization. To find out how, call the alumni association, the admissions office, or the office of student life. A parents' organization will keep you informed about what's happening on campus and the dates of family events. If there is no organization, contact the alumni association about starting one. Most likely you'll also find that there are specialized organizations for Greek houses, band parents, and so on. Rest assured, your child will appreciate your involvement. You'll also be surprised by how many conversations you'll strike up with other parents. You might also find you have opportunities to make contributions of time or money to your child's college, department, or social or academic organization. But be careful not to encroach on your child's turf, and check with them first.

Stay in Touch

Both you and your child will want to stay in touch – more or less often depending on your child and your communication style. It goes without saying that your child should have all the contact information of all the people they or you would want them to stay in touch with – you (at home and work), siblings, grandparents, extended family, friends, and anyone else you think of.

My first rule for staying in touch is simply to be available, whether it's by phone, e-mail, or text message. Before your child heads off to school, it's a good idea to make sure they'll have reliable cell phone service; if they're headed to more rural locations, you might have to look into local carriers and services. Don't expect the best service in your hometown to be the best at your child's school.

My second rule is that when they call, LISTEN TO THEM! With all the new things going on in their life, they'll want and need to talk. Ask about people, places, what

they like and don't like; invite and allow them to express their views and opinions about school or just life in general.

If you hope your child will write, you can get the motor running by giving them a stack of stamped or prepaid postcards with your address already filled in. You might even consider doing this with a stack of the school's postcards. All they'll have to do is write out a short note and drop it in the mail. If they run out, replenish the supply. You can do the same thing with Grandma's address or the address of someone who funded a scholarship your child received.

You should also make it a point to write to them. Believe it or not, they will appreciate hearing from you and probably get a confidence boost. My dad wrote this letter my freshman year of college in 1984. I include it because it made me feel good, and it's a good example for other parents. You can probably tell from the fact that I still have it that it means a great deal to me.

Dec. 4

LANCE,

I AM WRITING THIS FROM WORK, SO IT WILL HAVE TO BE SHORT. THE PICTURES TURNED OUT PRETTY WELL, SO WE WANTED YOU TO HAVE THEM AT SCHOOL. (BILL HAS SOME DIFFERENT ONES)

I DEPOSITED YOUR CHECK FROM GRANDAD. IF YOU HAVE ANY MORE DIFFICULTY WITH FUNDS, JUST LET ME KNOW.

YOUR MOM AND I ARE LOOKING FORWARD TO HAVING YOU HOME AT CHRISTMAS. WE STILL ARE NOT USED TO HAVING SUCH A QUIET HOUSE. I KNOW YOU PLAN ON WORKING, BUT IT WILL STILL BE NICE TO HAVE YOU AT HOME.

WE BOTH KNOW THAT YOU ARE NOT MAKING AS GOOD GRADES AS YOU WANT TO (OR AS YOU CAN), BUT WE UNDERSTAND THE DIFFICULTIES AND ADJUSTMENTS THAT HAVE TO BE MADE DURING THE FIRST YEAR. WORK HARD AND DO THE BEST YOU CAN. WE ARE PULLING FOR YOU.

GOOD LUCK SON — SEE YOU IN A COUPLE OF WEEKS.

LOVE,
DAD.

While we're talking about mail – be sure to send your child stuff. It's especially welcome at crunch times like finals week. Ship them goodie bags, cookies, newspaper clippings from home, socks, a sweater, or whatever is appropriate. They'll be excited to get a package, and they and their dorm or suite mates will appreciate the food you send.

It's been my experience that female college students usually stay in closer touch than males do. Don't be surprised and don't get mad when your child doesn't return telephone calls or digital messages right away. Figure out a way to let them know when you REALLY need to talk right away. Otherwise let them do things in their own time – likely in the middle of the night!

Visit them at school only when you both agree and they invite you. If you surprise them by dropping by, you could be the one getting the surprise. Most schools plan moms, dads or parents weekends at least once a year, sometimes every semester. If invited, you should go, whether or not you're interested in the sport, variety show, or other event it centers around. It will be time spent together, and their time to introduce you to their new world and friends. Oh, and don't be surprised if one of the weekend activities is buying them food, clothes, and other necessities of college life.

Encourage your student to stay at school rather than come home every weekend. They need to connect with their new environment and build an on-campus support network. It's difficult to do either if they spend every weekend at home. And nearly all student affairs specialists will tell you that staying on campus will make them more successful and more likely to stay in school.

When they do come home, don't expect them to act the same way they did before they left. They may dress a little differently, speak differently or use new words,

TIP

Encourage your student to stay at school rather than come home every weekend.

listen to different music, be trying out a new look, be more interested in politics, or question things they didn't question before. Don't expect the same rules to apply that were appropriate when they were in high school. Discuss new ground rules – what hour to be home at night, how and when to contact you if their plans change, when they won't be home for dinner, if friends can come over and under what circumstances. Remember, at college they're used to having no rules at all.

Also be sure to take advantage of their visits home. It's the best time – and the only time – for you to communicate face-to-face. They probably appreciate the chance to get back to the real world of human interaction and escape from the electronic world they live in most the time. Also, remind your collegian that their younger brothers or sisters will appreciate a little of their time too.

Let Them Learn

In college, your child will likely receive academic advising that is delivered using a developmental advising philosophy. This means that their advisor will help them not only with academic planning, goal setting, and career counseling, but also with developing and growing as an individual by learning to articulate their wants and needs, seeking information, taking action to solve their own problems, advocating for themselves, and utilizing available resources. Other than home, no place compares to college when it comes to learning essential skills for life.

Your child is learning to be self-sufficient. For the first time, you might find that you have to allow them to mess up or fail. They won't learn how to fix mistakes if they're not allowed to make them. A finance charge or hot check isn't the end of the world. When a problem arises at school, DO NOT go to campus and fix it for them. Help your child figure out where to find a solution and talk them through the steps to fix it, but make them learn from the experience. Get involved only as a last resort – when they've tried and cannot fix the problem.

If they have academic difficulties, be constructive, not punitive. Help them figure out what to do next time to avoid the same pitfalls. Encourage them to find people and campus resources whose business is providing help. In my experience, short-term academic problems usually don't result from lack of effort. More often, students are just a little overwhelmed by complex situations or confused about what's required. A visit to a professor or academic advisor is often all that's needed to resolve the issue. Longer-term problems like poor grades over more than a semester often have deeper causes. In these cases, parents will most likely need to get involved.

Private Information

Federal law protects the privacy of your child's academic records. Once your child starts school, you will not receive or have access to any information regarding their grades. Their teachers and advisors cannot talk with you about their grades. Only your child can grant you permission to see those records. They can do so formally by signing a written release granting you access to their records. If you suspect a problem and you want to know your child's grades, you'll have to get your child to cooperate.

Keep Learning

Okay, so now you've read this book. Is that all you need to know? Not quite. In fact, not at all. There are two valuable resources you really should investigate:

▶ The CollegePrep-101 web site, located at **www.collegeprep101.com**
▶ The College Answer Guy web site, at **www.collegeanswerguy.com**.

Visit these sites and continue your quest for every piece of information available on preparing for, getting into, and succeeding in college.

CollegePrep-101, launched in 1996, is home to tons more information – academic advice from a professor, a glossary of college terms, diaries and journals from college students, information about majors, diversity, stress, and disabilities – to name just a few of the topics. I invite you visit and learn to your heart's content.

College Answer Guy is quickly becoming a go-to source for quick, useful advice on the college selection, application, and transition processes. It's home is to a college prep blog and podcasts for those of you in the digital generation. If you're more old school, you can find College Answer Guy columns published in a growing number of regional newspapers.

In addition to my two web sites, I'd strongly encourage you to find and peruse the Occupational Outlook Handbook (OOH) at **www.bls.gov/oco**. Put out by the U.S. Department of Labor, the OOH maintains TONS of information about virtually every career path a person could be interested in, including job descriptions, education requirements, working conditions, salary data, career outlook, and much more. It's a great, unbiased resource I always refer my students to when they're searching for job or career information.

I appreciate you're reading my book, invite you to utilize my web sites, and encourage you to share them with others. I'd also be thrilled to hear about your experiences taking the big step to college selection and get your feedback regarding the information I've provided. Feedback forms on both the CollegePrep-101 and College Answer Guy web sites make it easy for you to contact me.

Additional copies of College Prep 101, in Adobe PDF ro hard copy, can be purchased on the CollegePrep-101 web site.

Thank you. I wish you good luck and good hunting....

About the
AUTHOR

Lance Millis, author of *College Prep 101*, is also the
creator/writer of two web resources for students
and families navigating the high-school-to-college
transition – **www.collegeprep101.com** and
www.collegeanswerguy.com. Millis has over eighteen
years experience in high school and college relations,
new student enrollment, freshman orientation, academic advisement, and student services administration at
Oklahoma State University. He has won awards for academic advising and for creating CollegePrep-101. Millis
holds BS and MS degrees from OSU and is a graduate
of Bartlesville High School, in Bartlesville, Oklahoma. In
college, he was a member of Delta Tau Delta Fraternity,
Phi Epsilon Kappa Honorary Fraternity, and served as
OSU's mascot, Pistol Pete, during his senior year. Millis is
married and has two children.

CREDITS

CREATIVE

Jean Erickson, Erickson Design
Art Director and Designer

Michael O'Neill, O'Neill Marketing Communications
Editor

PHOTOGRAPHY/IMAGES

Cover image: ©iStockphoto.com/Che McPherson; Chapter page and folio icons: ©iStockphoto.com/ Tom Nulens; Chapter heading textures: ©iStockphoto.com/naphtalina; Most pages: Energy path photos ©iStockphoto.com/Duncan Walker; Page 5: Photo © iStockphoto.com/Trista Weibell; Page 6: Photo © iStockphoto.com/Eliza Snow; Page 7: Photo © iStockphoto.com/Jacom Stephens; Page 9, 74: Photos ©iStockphoto.com/Viorika Prikhodko; Page 10: Photo © iStockphoto.com/Carol Gering; Pages 10-16 background image: Photo © iStockphoto.com/Rafa Irusta; Page 11: Photo © iStockphoto.com/ Diego Cervo; Page 12: Photo © iStockphoto.com/Nicholas Monu; Page 13: Photo © iStockphoto.com/ Aldo Murillo; Page 13, 70: Photos © iStockphoto.com/Sean Locke; Page 14, 32, 76, 83: Photos © iStockphoto.com/RichVintage; Page 16: Photo © iStockphoto.com/ericsphotography; Page 17: Photo © iStockphoto.com/Guillermo Perales Gonzalez; Page 18, 55: Photos © iStockphoto.com/Skip O'Donnell; Page 19: Photo © iStockphoto.com/g_studio; Page 20: Photo © iStockphoto.com/Chad Anderson; Page 21: Photo © iStockphoto.com/MACIEJ NOSKOWSKI; Page 22: Photo © iStockphoto.com/Andrey Shiryaev; Page 22: Photo © iStockphoto.com/Laurence Gough; Page 25: Photo © iStockphoto.com/ bluestocking; Page 26, 81: Photos © iStockphoto.com/Pali Rao; Page 27, 90: Photos © iStockphoto.com/Stefan Klein; Page 29: Photo © iStockphoto.com/Tilmann von Au; Page 31, 64, 69, 80, 82: Photos ©iStockphoto.com/Jacob Wackerhausen; Page 35: Photo © iStockphoto.com/Joshua Blake; Page 36: Photo © iStockphoto.com/TriggerPhoto; Page 37: Photo © iStockphoto.com/John Miller (UCLA); Page 38: Photo courtesy/Oklahoma State University; Page 39: Photo © iStockphoto.com/Forest Woodward; Page 40: Photo courtesy /University of Missouri; Page 42: Photo © iStockphoto.com/Arman Davtyan; Page 45: Photo © iStockphoto.com/David H. Lewis; Page 47: Photo © iStockphoto.com/starfotograf; Page 50: Photo © iStockphoto.com/Amanda Rohde; Page 53: Photo © iStockphoto.com/Stephanie Phillips; Page 56, 59, 63, 67, 89, 95: Photos ©iStockphoto.com/Kevin Russ; Page 61: Photo © iStockphoto.com/Maartje van Caspel; Page 66: Photo © iStockphoto.com/Luca di Filippo; Page 68: Photo © iStockphoto.com/walik; Page 72: Photo © iStockphoto.com/Peter Finnie; Page 73: Photo © iStockphoto.com/Yanni Raftakis; Page 75: Photo © iStockphoto.com/Millanovic; Page 79: Photo © iStockphoto.com/digitalskillet; Page 81: Photo © iStockphoto.com/Pali Rao; Page 84: Photo © iStockphoto.com/Roberta Osborne; Page 86: Photo © iStockphoto.com/Sharon Dominick; Page 90: Photo © iStockphoto.com/Stefan Klein; Page 91: Photo © iStockphoto.com/Brad Killer; Page 97: Photo © iStockphoto.com/Daniela Andreea Spyropoulos; Page 101: Photo courtesy/Lance Millis.

THANKS

The author, designer, and editor wish to thank Stillwater National Bank for underwriting this edition and publication of *College Prep 101*.